FAUST AND THE PADSHAH SPHINX:
RESHAPING THE NATO ALLIANCE TO WIN IN AFGHANISTAN

> [If we are united in purpose], we shall possess the strength of a Giant and there will be none who can make us afraid. Divided, and we shall become weak; a prey to intrigues and internal discord.[1]
>
> —General George Washington, 15 May, 1796

The NATO led multinational mission in Afghanistan faces challenges that inhibit its ability to accomplish the mission. To remedy this, NATO must undertake a concerted effort to identify these challenges and provide solutions. Amongst the challenges NATO faces is a lack of unity of effort, divergent political wills, national caveats, and divergent US and European reactions to the complex Afghan strategic environment. This Strategic Research Paper (SRP) defines the challenges both NATO and the US face and identifies the remedies. These range from developing leaders who understand NATO, establishing unity of effort, employing troop contributing nations in areas where they are best utilized, and deploying the NATO Response Force (NRF). Perhaps the most important ingredient for success is having strategic leaders with the tact, will and skill to create an environment where the alliance can succeed in Afghanistan.

Background – How Did We Get Here?

After the rout of the Taliban Regime in the winter of 2001-2002, the US maintained a small military footprint in Afghanistan. These forces concentrated largely on counter-terrorism operations against Al Qaeda. Their mission gradually transformed to nation building, but still with a small American force commitment. To sustain this evolving reconstruction and development effort, the United States solicited support from the North Atlantic Treaty Organization (NATO). NATO provided force packages to support the nation building endeavor beginning in December 2001, which became in 2003 the International Security Assistance Force (ISAF). NATO understood the mission to be peacekeeping and security for aid agencies bringing relief. By all appearances, Afghanistan seemed stable, with even the now contentious HELMAND Province reporting few significant activities (SIGACTs) as late as 2005.[2]

The plan for ISAF was to assume security over the entire nation, allowing the US force commitment to shrink. ISAF started by taking over security for Regional Command (RC) Capital (Kabul region) in 2003, RC North in 2004, RC West in 2005, RC South in July 2006 finally RC East in October 2006. To assist in transitioning the mission to ISAF, the United States (US), and its Coalition partners, conducted a series of operations in the more contentious areas of the Afghan countryside to pacify the regions before they transitioned to ISAF control. There were challenges, but the plan progressed.

Everything changed in 2006 when a resurgent Taliban emerged in southern and eastern Afghanistan. This was a result of the lack of US ground forces in 2001 to prevent the Taliban's hard-core leadership from escaping into Pakistan's Federally Administered Tribal Areas (FATA).[3] The Taliban leadership used 2002-2005 to reconstitute their ranks from the radical Madrassas of the area. The recruitment, retraining and reconstitution phase ended in early 2006 as the Taliban launched their offensive into Afghanistan from their sanctuaries in Pakistan.[4]

The fighting was particularly brutal in RC South, where Canadian, UK, Dutch, US, and Danish forces faced a series of concerted attacks from insurgents led by the Quetta Shura Taliban. In April 2006, the Taliban launched their "spring offensive" with surprising tenacity. By September, the Taliban operated in company and battalion sized formations and assumed a conventional approach to their campaign. The focal point of their attacks was against the Kandahar, Panjwai, Zahri Districts, with an eye on cutting off the south from RC East and RC Capital. The Canadians led a valiant counterattack against the Taliban during the first two-weeks of September 2006. The Operation (OP), called Medusa, relied heavily on airpower and, after heavy ground fighting, succeeded in thwarting the Taliban campaign.

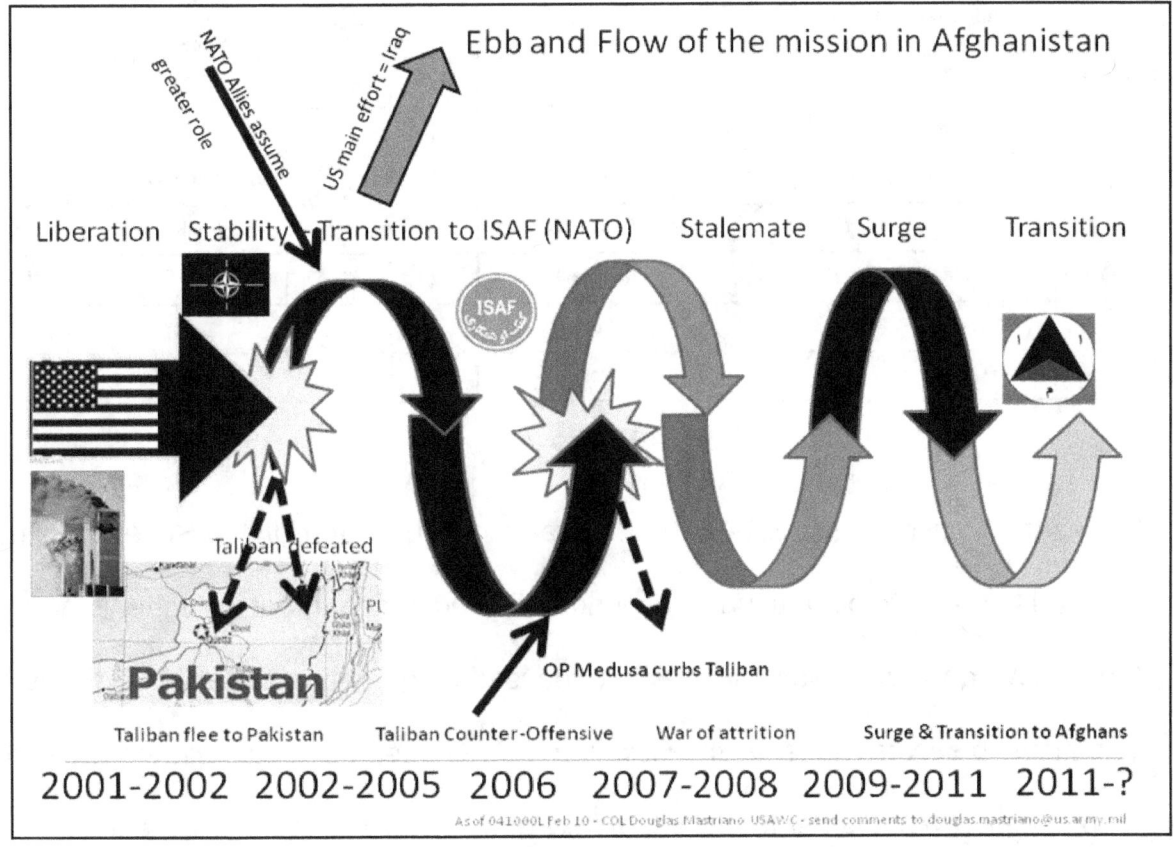

Figure 1.

Although OP Medusa was a tactical victory, it had several shortcomings. Due to a lack of both NATO forces and trained Afghan National Security Forces (ANSF), the Taliban escaped to fight another day. Elements of the Taliban infiltrated back into the contested districts (although in much smaller numbers) only weeks after OP Medusa.

3

Nevertheless, the unease coming out of Medusa was the realization among NATO nations that ISAF was more than peacekeeping.

	Nation	Troops		Nation	Troops		Nation	Troops
	Albania	255		Georgia	175		Portugal	105
	Armenia	0		Germany	4415		Romania	945
	Australia	1550		Greece	15		Singapore	40
	Austria	2		Hungary	315		Slovakia	240
	Azerbaijan	90		Iceland	3		Slovenia	70
	Belgium	575		Ireland	8		Spain	1070
	Bosnia & Herzegovina	10		Italy	3150		Sweden	410
	Bulgaria	540		Jordan	0		The Former Yugoslav Republic of Macedonia'	165
	Canada	2830		Latvia	175		Turkey	1755
	Croatia	295		Lithuania	165		Ukraine	8
	Czech Republic	440		Luxembourg	9		United Arab Emirates	25
	Denmark	750		Netherlands	1940		United Kingdom	9500
	Estonia	150		New Zealand	220		United States	47085
	Finland	95		Norway	500			
	France	3750		Poland	1955		Total	85795

Figure 2.

As this transpired in 2005-2006, the strategic focus of the United States was Iraq and militarily unable to operationally respond to this emerging threat in Afghanistan. To fill the security gap, US diplomatic pressure focused on garnering more NATO force contributions to secure Afghanistan. However, NATO troop contributing nations did not sign up to fight a war. Rather than immediately offer up new forces, many nations reverted to defensive solutions. In fact, some nations providing additional forces, attached restrictive national caveats on their deploying units that forbade field commanders from engaging in active combat missions. These restrictions created an environment that allowed insurgents and others to exploit a security void.

4

Today, there are forty-three nations supporting the ISAF mission in Afghanistan, but few permit their Soldiers to participate in offensive combat. This frustrates US forces who mockingly label ISAF as "I Suck At Fighting." With so many restrictions or strings attached, can the United States rely upon their NATO Allies in Afghanistan? Without a unified effort, can NATO get the job done?

What is at stake for the United States in the ISAF mission? The US National Security Strategy and the National Defense Strategy highlight the following interests in Afghanistan and, by extension, are related to the NATO led ISAF mission:

- Winning the counterinsurgency in Afghanistan & stabile Afghan government[5]

- Stabile region (specifically Pakistan)[6]

- Preservation of NATO[7]

- International credibility vis-à-vis the War on Terror[8]

The United States is gambling both its own and NATO's credibility with these interests in Afghanistan. This gamble goes beyond any argument of sunk costs over the last nine years and centers on the ramifications of failure. Failure will embolden Islamic radicals and result in Afghanistan's collapse into civil war. Catastrophe in Afghanistan will also trigger the radicalization of Pakistan's Federally Administered Tribal Areas (FATA) and failure of NATO's first out of area mission. If these come to fruition, the Alliance's demise is certain. How does NATO and the US forces succeed?

Defining the Mission: What is the United States' desired end-state in Afghanistan? Is it to win the counterinsurgency? Or, is it the preservation of NATO? The United States must succeed with both. The United States asked its Allies to fill the security void during our 2003-2009 operations in Iraq and they made considerable commitments in support of this request. With this in mind, the US has three options related to both winning the counterinsurgency and preserving NATO: 1) proceed in Afghanistan without NATO, 2) the status quo – no changes to application of NATO forces in ISAF or 3) continue with NATO in Afghanistan, but make key adjustments. [9]

Option #1 - Go forward in Afghanistan without NATO or the cut your losses option. A US led coalition is in many ways easier. At the operational and tactical level it provides better unity of command and effort in the execution of the mission. However, we would not have as many forces in Afghanistan. The NATO led ISAF mission provides approximately 40,000 of the 86,000 troops in the ISAF mission. [10] This is half of all ISAF forces. By cutting NATO out, and, by extension, most of ISAF, the USA will inherit a far greater burden financially, logistically and militarily. Without NATO, the US would assume the security of Regional Commands North, West, South and Capital now provided by largely non-USA NATO forces. Today, we benefit from this arrangement with the economy of force allowing the US to focus on the more contentious areas of the area of operations (AO).

The international nature of ISAF also provides legitimacy to the mission. This dispels judgments that the USA is empire building. The US loses this if NATO departs the theater. Furthermore, ISAF nations provide considerable economic aid, reconstruction and development. Including NATO assures the linkage of both a physical presence and financial investment in the success of this mission. These two motivators are not mutually exclusive. The financial commitment to nation building of a donor nation in Afghan will shrink considerably without a military presence on the ground. It's no secret; the coffers of the United States cannot afford to replace any of these shortfalls – troops or money.

Optional #2 - Status Quo – no changes to use of NATO in ISAF. This option portends that if NATO can muddle through the mission, over time, it will prevail. The construct of the mission, the lack of unity of command (and effort) is inefficient and can only succeed with unlimited time and no reduction of resources. Even under perfect conditions, success is doubtful in this course of action. Furthermore, several key nations supporting the NATO led ISAF mission have weak political will (hence the many national caveats tying the hands of their deployed forces). The longer the mission continues, the more likely that battle losses will motivate a nation to retreat from the mission. If this does occur, it will levy a major psychological blow to both NATO and the United States. The status quo option also condones the inefficiencies that exist in ISAF. This includes the additional layers of command and control, and duplicative organizations. The status quo option is better suited for a conventional war of attrition, than for the political realities of the resourced constrained ISAF mission.

Option #3 – Continue with NATO in Afghanistan, but revise the fundamentals. NATO was created for a specific strategic objective and is struggling to adjust to the unique challenges it faces in Afghanistan. NATO's foundation in 1949 began with twelve countries; ten European, the USA, and Canada. The purpose of the alliance, according to NATO's first Secretary General, Lord Ismay, was "to get the United States in, keep the Soviets out and keep the Germans down."[11] Now, twenty-eight nations strong, NATO is in Afghanistan, in the midst of one of the most complex situations it has faced.

NATO recently adopted a series of transformations to make it more versatile and relevant for the post Cold War world. This includes the development of the NATO Response Force (NRF) able to deploy within five days upon notification to a contingency operation. However, the old processes and structures of the Cold War era remain in place. Before the NRF can deploy, it must garner the consent of the member nations. For instance, the NRF was available to deploy to help the hard-pressed Canadians in Kandahar Province in 2006. It never happened solely because consensus was not possible. Also, many of the NATO national armies are better equipped and trained for a conventional war which does not translate to a counterinsurgency force. So, although NATO members are now moving to increase their "burden sharing" in Afghanistan, the dilemma is these forces are not all suited for a counterinsurgency fight.[12]

Addressing NATO's shortcomings is a long-term venture and ought to coincide with its continued support of the ISAF mission. NATO needs to invest in counter-insurgency training and appropriately outfit a portion of their forces to support this mission. The US can do much to encourage this effort. NATO must also carefully review the troop contribution by its diverse donors and assign them to regions and functions in Afghanistan where they can operate with the most efficiency and effectiveness. Some of member nations have niche skills which need to be leveraged to NATO's advantage in ISAF. Yet, the issue is the willingness of member nations to fully commit and, within their capacity, to do their part. ISAF is NATO's top priority, but many of the nations refuse to increase their force commitment in Afghanistan. If the alliance is to remain credible and win, placing the properly trained forces in the proper mission and reconciling the books on forces is fundamental.

Whether the Alliance or... Coalition?

General Dwight Eisenhower said that:

America's transformation... from a situation of appalling danger to unparallel might in battle was one of the two miracles that [compelled the Germans] to surrender on May 7, 1945. The other was the development... of near perfection in allied conduct of war operations.[13]

General Eisenhower credits the alliance as one of the reasons of our victory over NAZI Germany in World War II. This highlights the power when nations come together in a common cause. Unfortunately, Eisenhower's experience is a historic anomaly. Coalitions and Alliances normally fail due to conflicting interests and divergent commitments. Eisenhower's victorious alliance was just a handful of nations, the United States, United Kingdom and the United Soviet Socialist Republics. Outside of these, the other partners were fragments of nations conquered by Hitler's Armies. Although challenging enough, it made his job easier than the one we face today in Afghanistan. The United States must navigate through the complexities of a difficult mission, with scores of nations, who have diverse interests.

Understanding an Alliance and Coalition. There is a basic misunderstanding of the differences between an alliance and coalition. Comprehending the differences is vital in that an alliance and coalition each have constraints unique to it. Joint Publication 0-2 (Unified Action Armed Forces) defines an alliance as "the result of formal agreements (i.e. treaties) between two or more nations for broad, long-term objectives which further the common interests of the members."[14] NATO is the example of this, where each of the twenty-eight members has an equal vote. This means that the smallest nation, with little to no support of the ISAF mission, can, on its own, veto a proposal set before the alliance.

On the other side is a coalition, which is "an ad hoc arrangement between two or more nations for common action."[15] Operation Desert Storm is an example of a coalition as the United States rallied international support to eject Saddam's forces from Kuwait. The nations in this coalition did not have an equal vote in the operation and generally fell under the United States, which planned and led the mission. In a coalition, the lead nation has more influence in making unilateral decisions. The opposite is true in the construct of the NATO Alliance.

Afghanistan is one of the most complex environments to combat. Its history, independent tribes, diverse ethnicities (Hazaaras, Pashtuns, Uzbeks and Tadjiks), porous borders, Islamic extremists, government corruption, little national infrastructure, lack of a national identity, opium and many other issues combine to make it a complicated mission. Adding to this equation is the complexity of having the NATO *Alliance* leading this mission comprised of an international *coalition* of troop contributing nations. This is a recipe for confusion and discord.

NATO's Challenges - Getting It Right

NATO is plagued by challenges and problems and the US is quick to point out these deficiencies. But, some of the problems are of the US's own making. The following shall discuss these challenges in some detail. It is not wise to either ignore or emphasize the deficiencies that plague NATO. Instead, all member nations, especially the US, must lead by example, uprightly, with virtue and put their collective houses in order in order to solve NATO's inadequacies. The following quote from the Gospel of

Matthew highlights the problem of pointing out another's shortcomings, while ignoring

your own:

> Why do you look at the speck of saw dust in your brother's eye and pay no attention to the plank in your own eye? How can you say to your brother "let me take the speck out of your eye"' When all the time there is a plank in your own eye? You hypocrite, first take the plank out of your own eye and then you will see clearly to remove the speck from your brother's eye.[16]

National Caveats. Of all the issues to contend with in NATO, national caveats are

the most problematic. These are restrictions the troop contributing nations place on

their forces – to wit, what they can and cannot do. Most of the nations contributing

troops impose some type of national caveat. These range from not conducting counter-

narcotics operations to staying in a restricted or defined area. National caveats

exemplify a nation's commitment and political will associated with the mission. The

biggest criticism by the US and the other nations involved in the contested regions of

Afghanistan are the national caveats that prevent the armed forces of key nations from

participating in combat. This lack of shared risk undermines the military aspect of the

ISAF mission.[17] Germany is the most criticized, which has its 4,400 plus soldiers

assigned to the "quiet" RC North. Critics say that the sizeable German presence would

be more useful in the contested RC SOUTH.[18] But given the national obstacles, it's not

possible. There are countless more such caveats that inhibit NATO. It's hard enough to

fight the enemy, but even harder when you cannot fully count on your friends.

Separate Formations are OK. It is regrettable that there are basically two groups

in ISAF; those who are authorized by their nations to conduct offensive combat, and

those who cannot. This poses a dilemma for the ISAF leadership and restricts what can

be done in the area of operations. However, resorting to criticism of this arrangement does nothing to solve the problem. All need to accept the fact that national caveats are mandates to ground forces from their respective capitals. Despite perhaps many of their Soldier's personal desire to do otherwise, the decisions of their national leadership is final. NATO needs to perform the mission analysis, determine how best to utilize these forces so they best support mission execution.

No Sacred Cows - NATO Response Force (NRF). The United States and other member nations must work with NATO to utilize all its assets in Afghanistan. Convincing all member nations to provide support and additional forces is difficult while NATO protects its own resource. The NRF is NATO's reaction force in time of war. NATO is at war. Why not employ it for a nine month mission in support of ISAF? It is hard to understand why NATO will not utilize this force to support the US surge, provide material evidence of NATO's commitment to the ISAF mission and offer a legitimate option for transitioning the theater from NATO to the Afghan National Security Forces (ANSF). Deploying the NRF to Regional Command SOUTH, without caveats, to participate in all missions for the complete campaign season is currently an option, but not one supported by contributing nations.

It will not be easy to convince NATO to allow its forces to serve in the contentious areas of Afghanistan. The key ingredient is a defined timeline for deployment, tied to achieving operationally important tasks as a bridge transitioning the mission from the US surge to the ANSF. The deployment of the NRF will send an unambiguous message of NATO's commitment to achieving their strategic objectives in Afghanistan. It also provides concrete evidence of the alliance's unity and demonstrates NATO's continued viability in the Post Cold World. The NRF's deployment will send a strong signal from NATO and give the nations seeking a graceful way out, the opportunity rethink their commitments and turn those displaying a lack of resolve.

Lacking Unity of Command and Effort. The unintended consequence of national caveats is that it undermines the mission's unity of effort by segregating nations into those who will and will not fight. This is a serious problem. However, this goes beyond our allies' national caveats. The US compounds this by having diverse and even redundant chains of command and duplicative functions that further confound the mission.

Afghanistan is in the Central Command (CENTCOM) Area of Responsibility (AOR) and requires reporting by US forces to the command and control headquarters in Tampa, Florida. Within the NATO Alliance, COMISAF also has a reporting chain to the Allied Supreme Commander (SACEUR) in Belgium. The SACEUR is also the European Command Commander in Stuttgart, Germany. Additionally, the US leads non-ISAF missions that fall under the Operation Enduring Freedom banner as a separate US independent effort. These layers of command confound unity of effort in an already difficult mission.

I came face to face with this confusing command and control arrangement during ISAF VIII, IX and X, while working in the ISAF CJ2. In this capacity, I worked theater wide intelligence assessments on behalf of the NATO led ISAF mission. Also performing the same exact job as the ISAF CJ2 in Kabul is the CENTCOM Joint Intelligence Operations Center-Afghanistan (JIOC-A). JIOC-A is a legacy organization from the US led the Afghan mission under Combined Forces Command-Afghanistan

(CFC-A). Instead of being absorbed into ISAF after the end of CFC-A operations, JIOC-A remained in place doing similar tasks as the ISAF CJ2 JIC.

Despite their commonality, the JIOC-A products were usually over classified, with only 10% of their products releasable to either ISAF or NATO.[19] This US centric capability bred suspicion amongst the allies and served to undercut NATO/ISAF CJ2 reporting. The net result with this approach is a lack of confidence and continuity with the intelligence effort in ISAF. This redundancy brings little of value to the mission and is just one of several examples where the US fosters a less than cooperative environment within the alliance construct.

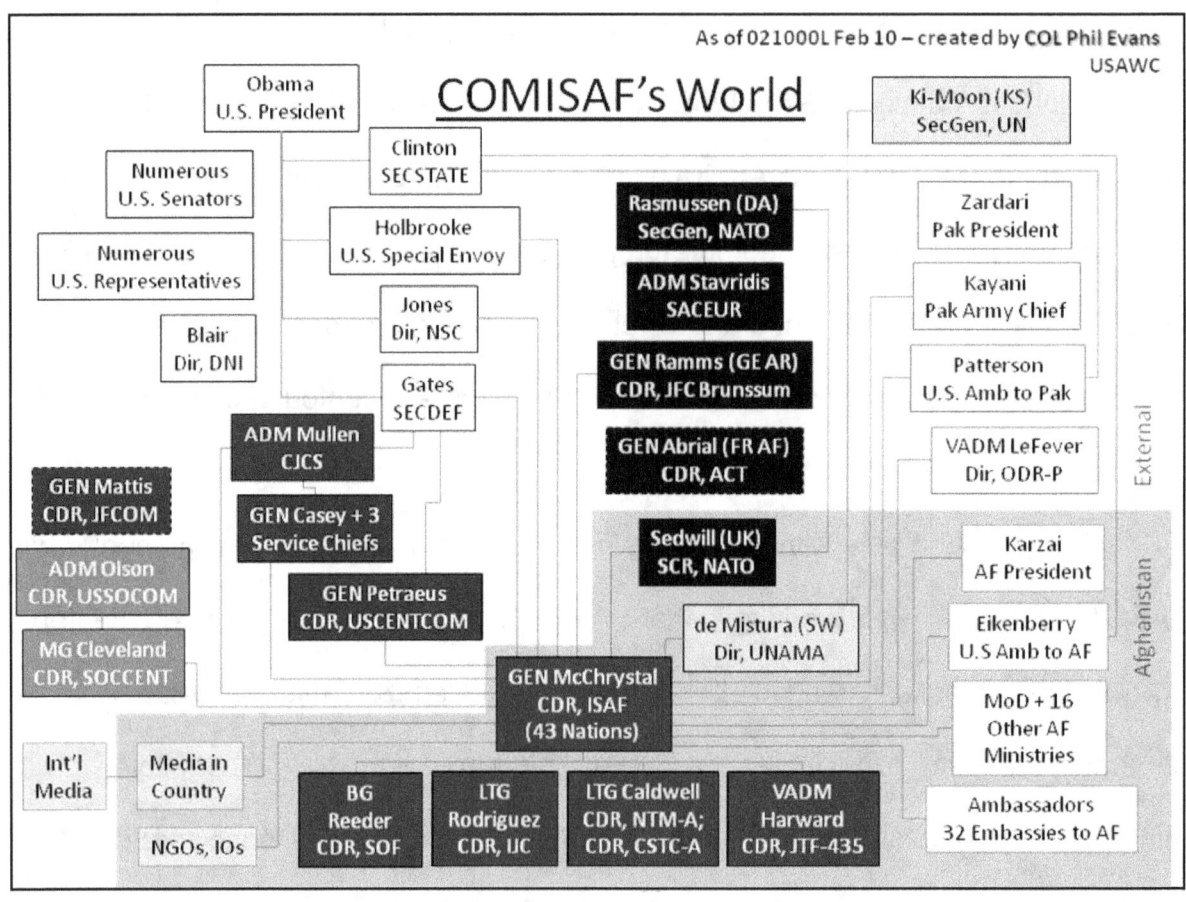

Figure 3.

This lack of unity of command is compounded by the need for common operating systems. There are five regional commands (RC Capital, North, West, South, and East) in Afghanistan. The RCs routinely use the ISAF operating systems except the US led RC East. How can one achieve unity of effort when the lead nation does not operate in the NATO communication systems? NATO's national caveats are a problem, but it is compounded by layers of extra US reporting chains, redundant and contradictory organizations and by not using the common operating system. One American analyst, working for a national agency, bragged "he was proud the he had not turned on the NATO computer in six-months."[20] NATO has many problems, but this approach is not helpful and indicative of the parochialism that is choking NATO.

Unhealthy Reactions to Working in NATO. Complicating all of these issues is the lack of leader fortitude to fix the deficiencies that corrupt the foundation of NATO's organizational culture. These issues all serve to poison relationships and destroy trust. Anders Fogh Rasmussen, the NATO Secretary General made the following observation on this issue:

> There is no doubt that the United States is an indispensable part of the [ISAF] mission; and all Allies respect the sacrifices that the United States has made. But talking down the European and Canadian contributions – as some here in the US do... can become a self-fulfilling prophesy... If they don't feel as if their efforts and sacrifices in NATO are recognized and valued, they will be less inclined to make those efforts and those sacrifices.[21]

Many American officers generally have one of two reactions when working in a unique NATO environment. One manifestation is the US-centric approach, while the other is to become a type of "Europhile." Either reaction is counterproductive and detracts from the mission.

The *US Centric or Guys like us Approach:* A common reaction of US officers is to be tribal and to associate and work with only those who are like us. This means that the in-crowd are native English speakers (Canada, UK, Australia, and USA = CANUKAUS). This "guys like us" approach is encouraged by the separate US reporting chain and the special "four-eyes" club that exists.[22] The perception by the other nations is the US only trusts CANUKAUS and only those countries are offered the important tasks. This alienates the non-native speakers, disrupts the ISAF team and diminishes our ability to accomplish the mission by polarizing nations into various levels of confidence.

Equally troubling are those leaders labeled as *EUROPHILES* or *gone native.* Although less common, there is a response by some to throw themselves completely into the European camp. Josephus Daniels, the Secretary of the Navy between 1913-1921, made the following statement on this affliction: "[there is a] peculiar malady which affects certain types of Americans who go abroad and become in many respects un-American" "[23]

These leaders and staff officers will tend to overlook European deficiencies and apologize for US shortcomings. Of the two, being US Centric is the most common and it undercuts the mission. The previous quote by NATO Secretary General Anders Fogh Rasmussen encapsulates the effects of such an attitude and the negative impact it has upon the alliance as a whole.

Neither of these extreme reactions is constructive and leaders must work diligently to build the team. Dignity and respect for others is a core value of the US Soldier and for the betterment of the mission, it's time for the US to live up to its own standard. It is not easy to lead such a diverse group, but when done properly, the results are marvelous.

Wanted, Strategic NATO Leaders – Experience a Must. NATO has a lot on its hands in Afghanistan; probably too much. The United States cannot execute the ISAF mission without the support of their NATO allies. A concerted effort must be undertaken by the NATO nations to develop the strategic leader competencies necessary to build leaders who can lead the alliance. The most important attribute for all, but especially US leaders, is to learn how to operate effectively in a multinational *alliance.* As previously noted, working in NATO is a unique experience. Unfortunately, many leaders in ISAF possess little valuable NATO experience and their ignorance is affecting the mission. *What's the solution – easy to see but hard to fix.*

The antiquated rules of the NATO alliance are not insurmountable obstacles to affect immediate change. NATO has plenty of issues and weaknesses but every alliance comes with baggage and difficulties. Every one of the problems NATO faces is tied to some parochial interest. Leadership can help this effort by eliminating lip service to the allies and independent action leading to distrust and devastating unanimity. All member nations are guilty of some form of caveat or exclusive requirement. The US is equally culpable of its own caveats. These range from independent combat operations, exclusive applications of force, segregated communication systems, and exclusive reporting. On many of these issues, the US must lead the solution and inspire others to follow. General Stanley A. McCrystal highlighted the importance of getting this right when he said;

We must significantly modify organizational structures to achieve better unity of effort... Transform ISAF... fostering stronger unity of effort across the international community.[24]

Fighting alongside allies is no easy endeavor, but when executed correctly their power may be insurmountable for any enemy. In Afghanistan, NATO has the world's most advanced armies fighting side-by-side. The challenge is the application of proper leadership and leveraging forces where and when they can best serve the unified effort. Despite national restrictions, their presence gives NATO, and thereby the US, the potential to economize forces. This enables NATO to mass the better equipped forces in the more complex and contentious areas. The challenge is to employ these controlled forces in a manner that allows them to operate to their fullest ability. More NATO forces are of course desirable and as much part of the ultimate solution as any US military surge.

An ideal solution to bolster unanimity is the deployment of the NATO Reaction Force (NRF) in 2012 to support the Afghan surge. The NRF brings with it significant military power with its 25,000 Soldiers and diverse capabilities. Their inclusion, serves as a "NATO Surge". If timed to arrive as the US begins to lower their force levels, NATO can create a significant symbol of increasing resolve to win. The NRF's deployment also assures synergy between persistent force application and transitioning to the Afghanistan National Security Force (ANSF). This option makes sense and is long overdue. It supports NATO's intent to transition the mission to ANSF and provides the material power to thwart either any military threats or national perceptions that the alliance is vulnerable.

Both US and NATO senior leadership will not garner continued support if they do not include their partners in strategy formulation and execution. There will be a time to execute US only missions, or publish US only intelligence assessments, although these should be by exception. All partners can offer a great deal in developing strategy, providing intelligence and executing operations. The distressing item is that fifty-six years of trust amongst some of NATO's partners is withering. These acts, regardless if they are a norm or anomaly, are caustic in an alliance where perception is everything. This does little to endear all partners at a time when NATO (and the US) needs to provide greater support to the mission.

The US can demonstrate goodwill and cooperation by eliminating legacy organizations from the CFC-A days. This includes anything that excludes certain allies and emboldens only CANUKAUS organizations. These organizations are redundant, exclusive, generates suspicion and deeply divisive. In this alliance, every nation brings something of value to the fight. If the US and all NATO players fail to appreciate this fact, they progress at their own peril.

It's time to eliminate exclusive gatherings and organizations and other practices utilized to isolate the many and designate the few as elite. Occasions when non-Americans are asked to leave the room, or when the "four- eyes"/ CANUKAUS community conducts exclusive meetings ought to be the exception and not the rule. There are prudent times to protect national sources and methods, but it ought not to be the norm.

Unfortunately, the exclusive approach remains a problem even as recently as September – October 2009. Few allies were included when a group planners and strategist meet in Kabul to outline a new approach to Afghanistan. In fact very few allies were invited to the most recent such gathering. According to a lead planner, there were no more than three or four non-American planners participating despite as many as forty-three available in ISAF.[25]

US forces can immediately address one critical area where exclusive meetings and organizations inhibit unity of effort in Afghanistan. The intelligence processes and C2 structure is the most visible place to affect a meaningful and lasting impact for clear change. Many of the intelligence reports circulating in Kabul today, and specifically the ones from US organizations, are over classified. Often, this is the result of the originator, who does not know the difference between the designation of "releasable to ISAF" or "releasable to NATO". For example, the JOIC-A routinely classifies 90% of their reports as not releasable to either ISAF or NATO. [26] This shortcoming rests squarely upon the shoulders of the leaders in the intelligence community who are happy to stay trapped in a series of parochial firewalls. Senior leaders must break these obstacles and promulgate intelligence appropriately. With the right organization, NATO can demonstrate trust and unity is possible throughout its entire C2 structure.

Although ISAF's Joint Intelligence Center (JIC) is the theater's fusion center for intelligence, the barriers between the other major intelligence agencies in theater and the National Intelligence Cells (NICs) undermines the effort to bring security and stability to the country. The default solution proposed by American experts is to create yet another organization to remedy the existing shortfalls. This is not the solution. NATO and ISAF do not more obstacles, they need less. It is time to "right-size" the organization by eliminating the US dominated CENTCOM JIOC-A (Joint Intelligence Operations Center-Afghanistan) and ISAF JIC (Joint Intelligence Center) and fuse their capabilities under the banner of a Unified Theater Intelligence Center (UTIC). These barriers hinder information sharing and timeliness, and create unnecessary duplication of effort and a skeptical climate.

The UTIC is not another intelligence shell game. Both the JIOC-A and ISAF JIC have analysts doing similar tasks. There is no need for two robust intelligence organizations doing the same job. The UTIC will support mission accomplishment by creating intelligence unity of effort and eliminating duplication of effort and redundancies. The basis for configuring the UTIC is to produce better intelligence for the commander by fusing information from all of NATO, the ISAF troop contributing nations and the Afghans. The UTIC will resemble an "Intelligence Village," serving as the single location to go for all intelligence needs. It will produce the most fused, and coordinated intelligence in theater. More importantly, it will foster cooperation among the nations, enhance all intelligence support and prove the alliance is connected by its most guarded resource – intelligence.

All of these solutions require competence and experience in NATO operations. At the most senior levels, this means a competent strategic NATO leader. How does a country develop such a leader? The obvious solution is to make compulsory service in a NATO unit or staff. The optimal sequence for career progression is initially as a junior field grade officer, preferably a Major, with a follow on or re-bluing assignment as a senior grade 06 or junior one star flag officer. An officer must serve in NATO to understand the character of its Soldiers, the challenges they face, and the difficulty of not working in one's native culture or language. I served with a senior US officer in ISAF X, who boasted of his NATO experience. This experience was not evident in his skills leading allies. Upon closer inspection, his "NATO" experience was three years in an

American Division in Germany. Bottom line, he had no NATO experience and seldom worked alongside anyone outside of his American unit.

The problem is all NATO nations lack officers with personal experiences that foster both understanding and trust. Committing to a NATO solution in which all develop leaders, via a cohort system as outlined above, is vital to destroying myopic or Europhile Soldiers. The current set of key leaders in ISAF possesses little or no experience. They rely on their limited coalition experience and believe it is similar enough to qualify them to lead an alliance. It is not and the dysfunction blatantly obvious in Afghanistan is ample attestation of their naiveté.

NATO, and particularly the US, must develop an alliance savvy strategic leader. They desperately need another General Eisenhower to rise from the ranks and to lead them forward. The Afghan experience illustrates they are painfully deficient in this regard. Until NATO and its strongest partners develop or find these leaders, they risk failure. NATO can wield a powerful combined and joint team able to "win" in Afghanistan, but it's virtually impossible without implementing serious changes. Unless they commit to finding and cultivating this dynamic leadership, the chances of succeeding continue to diminish.

Conclusion

Nine years after the 9/11 attacks, things look grim in Afghanistan, but it is not too late. NATO, and her strongest partner, the US, possess both the initiative and ability to turn things around. The first step is to establish unity of effort and unity of command through competent strategic leadership. Everyone needs to appreciate their partner's contributions, agree to employ forces where they appropriately suit the mission, develop C2 structure to increase effectiveness and mutually support all members of the alliance to achieve the stated end state. No one, two or even three nations can do everything and expect to succeed, but cooperatively this alliance can win.

What is at stake in Afghanistan for NATO and the United States? It is hard to imagine a positive outcome with failure. Apocalypse like scenarios seem probable if things go terribly wrong. Failure of the ISAF mission will fragment NATO, with American influence in Europe diminishing in the face of an emerging EU army and its potential economic power. Afghanistan will certainly collapse into a failing state in a vicious civil war, dragging with it, the nuclear and fragile Pakistan. Emboldening radical Islamists, now gaining inspiration from the defeat of the last superpower, will likely stimulate additional struggles and destabilize more fragile states. This is not an outcome palatable to NATO, the US or the global community. They simply must do the hard work to create unity of effort and unity of command through capable leadership because loosing is not an option.

Endnotes

[1] Jared Sparks, The Writings of George Washington, (New York; Harper & Brothers, 1848).

[2] SIGACTs are events used by ISAF to measure the security of an area. SIGACTs include Improvised Explosive Devices (IEDs, small arms fires, simple attacks, complex attacks, surface to air fire, cache discoveries, kidnappings, indirect fire (usually a rocket fired at a compound), night letters (letters threatening someone for supporting the government), burning of schools, etc.

[3] Graham Usher, "The Pakistan Taliban," *Middle East Report,* 15 February 2007.

[4] Sharmeen Obaid-Chinoy, Pakistan: The New Taliban, FRONTLINE, 21 December 2007. http://www.pbs.org/frontlineworld/blog/2007/12/pakistan_the_ra.html

[5] *US National Security Strategy,* Washington, DC, March 2006, 12-13 and *National Defense Strategy,* Department of Defense, June 2008, introduction by President George Bush, 8,17.

[6] *US National Security* Strategy, Washington, DC, March 2006, 12-13 and *National Defense Strategy,* Department of Defense, June 2008, 8,17.

[7] *US National Security Strategy*, Washington, DC, March 2006, 20-21, 35.

[8] *US National Security Strategy*, Washington, DC, March 2006, 7-8, 12-13, 35 and *National Defense Strategy*, Department of Defense, June 2008, 1, 8,17.

[9] Several points discussed in the options portion of this paper are highlighted in the following article: Stanley R. Sloan, "Why should we think NATO can survive Afghanistan," *Program in Arms Control, Disarmament and International Security*, (University of Illinois, Urbana-Champaign, IL, 2008), 3-6.

[10] These troop numbers are current as of 22 October 2009 and provided by the NATO Joint Forces Command, Brunnsum (JFC-B), Netherlands. JFC-B is NATO's lead headquarters for the ISAF mission. Website: http://www.nato.int/isaf/docu/epub/pdf/placemat.html

[11] Ryan C. Hendrickson, "NATO's missions beyond Afghanistan," *Program in Arms Control, Disarmament and International Security*, (University of Illinois, Urbana-Champaign, IL, 2008), 7-9.

[12] Paul F. Diehl, "Problem with NATO Peace Keeping Missions," *Program in Arms Control, Disarmament and International Security*, (University of Illinois, Urbana-Champaign, IL, 2008), 10-13.

[13] Dwight D. Eisenhower, Crusade in Europe, (Garden City, NY: Doubleday, 1948), 4.

[14] Unified Action Armed Forces (UNAAF), Joint Publication 0-2, 10 July 2001, GL-4.

[15] Unified Action Armed Forces (UNAAF), Joint Publication 0-2, 10 July 2001, GL-5.

[16] Matthew 7:3-5

[17] Timo Noetzel and Sibylle Scheipers, "Coalition Warfare in Afghanistan: Burden sharing or Disunity?" Briefing Paper, Chatham House: Royal Institute of International Affairs," October 2007.

[18] Vincent Morelli, "NATO in Afghanistan: a Test of the Transatlantic Alliance," (Washington, DC: Congressional Research Service, August 2009), 10-11.

[19] This is based upon the authors experience in the later portion of ISAF X, when JIOC-A reporting this statistic to the CJ2.

[20] This occurred at the SHAPE Afghanistan Intelligence Conference, Krakow, Poland, May 2008.

[21] Anders Fogh Rasmussen, "Afghanistan and NATO: The Way Forward," 28 September 2009.

[22] Due to a bilateral intelligence sharing agreements, the USA has special intelligence release arrangements with several nations.

[23] Edward M. Coffman, The War to End All Wars, (Lexington, Kentucky: University Press of Kentucky, 1998), 105.

[24] Stanley A. McChrystal, *COMISAF's Initial Assessment,* ISAF Headquarters, Kabul, 30 August 2009, p. 1-3, 2-1.

[25] Based upon a conversation I had with one of the planners in late 2009.

[26] This is based upon the authors experience in the later portion of ISAF X, when JIOC-A reporting this statistic to the CJ2.